GRAPHIC HEROES OF THE AMERICAN REVOLUTION

THOMAS JEFFERSON

AND THE DECLARATION OF INDEPENDENCE

BY GARY JEFFREY

ILLUSTRATED BY EMANUELE BOCCANFUSO

Gareth Stevens
Publishing

Please visit our website, www.garethstevens.com.
For a free color catalog of all our high-quality books,
call toll free 1-800-542-2595 or fax 1-877-542-2596.

Library of Congress Cataloging-in-Publication Data

Jeffrey, Gary.
Thomas Jefferson and the Declaration of Independence / Gary Jeffrey.
p. cm. — (Graphic heroes of the American Revolution)
Includes index.
ISBN 978-1-4339-6026-0 (pbk.)
ISBN 978-1-4339-6027-7 (6-pack)
ISBN 978-1-4339-6025-3 (library binding)
1. Jefferson, Thomas, 1743-1826—Juvenile literature. 2. United States.
Declaration of Independence—Juvenile literature. 3. Presidents—United
States—Biography—Juvenile literature. 4. Statesmen—United States—
Biography—Juvenile literature. 5. United States—History—Revolution,
1775-1783—Biography—Juvenile literature. I. Title.
E332.79.J44 2011
973.4'6092—dc22
[B]
2011004701

First Edition

Published in 2012 by
Gareth Stevens Publishing
111 East 14th Street, Suite 349
New York, NY 10003

Copyright © 2012 David West Books

Designed by David West Books
Editor: Ronne Randall

Printed in China

CPSIA compliance information: Batch #DS11GS: For further information contact Gareth Stevens, New York, New York at 1-800-542-2595.

CONTENTS

WORDS OF REASON

In April 1775, the simmering tension between Britain and its American colonies boiled over into a pitched battle. At the Second Continental Congress, anti-British leaders called that they should go for broke and fight for outright independence.

The first clash between British and American forces took place on April 19, on Lexington Green, Massachusetts.

IT'S COMMON SENSE

Separating from Britain was unthinkable for many leaders at the congress. They wanted to fight a limited war to gain rights but stay part of the British Empire. The die-hard patriots had to work very hard to get support for their cause.

Benjamin Franklin called early for independence.

COMMON SENSE;
INHABITANTS
OF
AMERICA,

The pamphlet "Common Sense" by Thomas Paine helped change people's opinions about independence during 1776.

The earliest known likeness of Thomas Jefferson. He was only 33 years old in 1776.

RENAISSANCE MAN

Jefferson was born to a well-respected Virginia family. He had an excellent education, including time at college. As a young man, he loved to study the classics and nature, and lived at home until he married in 1772. A successful lawyer and local politician, Jefferson was a poor public speaker, but brilliant at drafting official documents. This talent and his passion for the patriot cause got him a seat at the Second Continental Congress. Jefferson was the second-youngest delegate there.

RESOLVE

"Put Virginia at the head of everything," said John Adams. Adams thought that where the largest and richest colony led, the rest would follow. Much had happened in the year since Lexington. The mood was different. It seemed the right time to put forward a bold resolution...

Lawyer John Adams was the mastermind of the patriot cause.

THOMAS JEFFERSON AND THE DECLARATION OF INDEPENDENCE

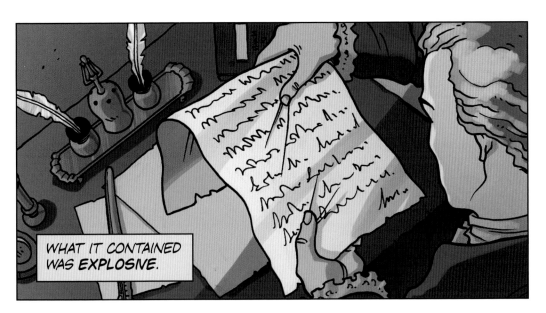

WHAT IT CONTAINED WAS **EXPLOSIVE.**

LEE HAD DRAFTED THE RESOLUTION ON THE ORDERS OF THE PATRIOT LEADERS OF VIRGINIA...

"... THAT THESE COLONIES ARE, AND OF RIGHT OUGHT TO BE, **FREE AND INDEPENDENT STATES!**."

GASP!

HEAR! HEAR!

AS LEE FINISHED SPEAKING, HIS COLLEAGUE THOMAS JEFFERSON LOOKED THE OTHER DELEGATES OVER.

NOT ALL OF THEM ARE YET **ALLOWED** TO VOTE ON INDEPENDENCE. I WAGER THE VOTE ON IT WILL BE **PUT OFF** UNTIL THEY GET **SUPPORT.**

AND SO IT WAS. BUT THE FEELING WAS THAT THE RESOLUTION **WOULD** BE SUPPORTED, SO...

...WE WILL ALL VOTE FOR FIVE MEMBERS TO FORM A COMMITTEE TO DRAFT A FORMAL **DECLARATION OF INDEPENDENCE!**

AMONG THE FIVE CHOSEN WERE JOHN ADAMS, BENJAMIN FRANKLIN, AND THOMAS JEFFERSON. ADAMS QUICKLY PROPOSED **ANOTHER** VOTE...

...TO CHOOSE WHO SHALL **WRITE** THE DOCUMENT.

MY VOTE IS FOR MR. JEFFERSON.

OH NO, I THINK **YOU** SHOULD DO IT, MR. ADAMS.

WELL, IF YOU ARE DECIDED, I WILL DO AS WELL AS I CAN.

JEFFERSON DIDN'T KNOW IT YET, BUT HIS ENTIRE LIFE SO FAR MADE HIM THE BEST PERSON FOR THE JOB.

VERY WELL! WHEN YOU HAVE DRAWN IT UP, WE WILL MEET.

JEFFERSON RENTED QUIET LODGINGS OUTSIDE THE CTY.

A PLACE WHERE HE COULD THINK IN PEACE.

MY STARTING POINT WILL BE MY OWN PROPOSED VIRGINIA CONSTITUTION...

...TO PUT THE CASE OF THE AMERICAN PEOPLE BEFORE THE WORLD.

THE MAIN PURPOSE OF THE DECLARATION WAS TO HELP CONGRESS GET AID FROM FOREIGN GOVERNMENTS.

SURROUNDED BY SCHOLARLY WORKS ON PHILOSOPHY AND HUMAN RIGHTS, JEFFERSON TOILED TO FIND HIS OWN WORDS, USING *HIS HEAD...*

...THAT ALL MEN ARE CREATED **EQUAL**, THAT THEY ARE ENDOWED WITH CERTAIN **UNALIENABLE** RIGHTS, THAT AMONG THESE ARE LIFE, LIBERTY, AND...

AND *HIS HEART...*

...THE PURSUIT OF **HAPPINESS.**

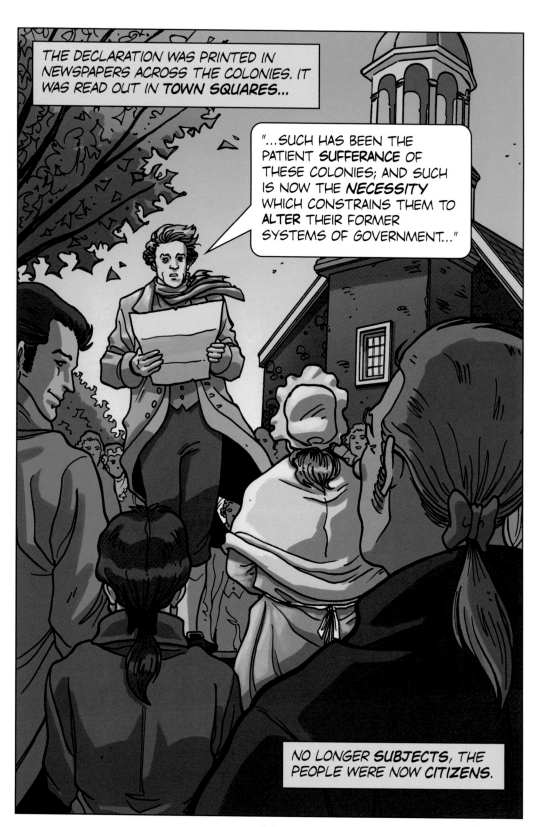

Jefferson's drafting of the Declaration was thought little more than routine during the war. The drafters of the Constitution didn't even use it. It was not until the 1790s, when Jefferson started a new political party, that the Declaration became a famous document.

By 1796, Jefferson had served America as an ambassador and secretary of state.

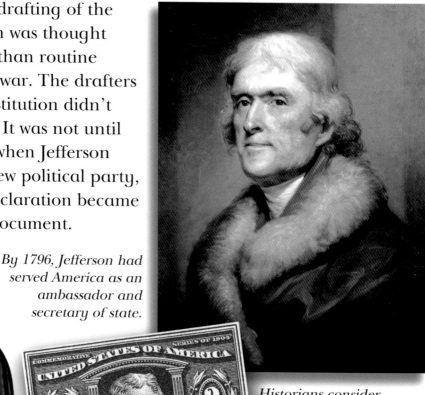

Historians consider Jefferson one of the great presidents. Here he is commemorated on a 1904 centenary stamp.

A memorial to Jefferson and his Declaration stands in Washington, DC. Both the man and the document are enduring icons of liberty for Americans.

PRESIDENT AND ICON

Jefferson became president in 1800 and served for two terms. He got rid of taxes and doubled the land area of the United States. In retirement, he founded the University of Virginia and went on living life to the full. Jefferson was nearly penniless when he died on July 4, 1826, aged 83.

GLOSSARY

clause A section of a legal document.

committee A group of people chosen to investigate and report or act on a matter.

constitution A document containing the fundamental laws and principles of a government or country.

constrain To compel or force someone to do something.

declaration A formal statement that is either written or oral.

delegate A person elected as a representative of another person or territory.

obnoxious To be extremely unpleasant or very annoying.

philosophy The study of the nature of reality, knowledge, or values based on logical reasoning and rational argument.

pledge To guarantee by a solemn, binding promise.

pursuit The act of chasing after or striving to get something.

resolution A formal statement of a decision or course of action.

simmering To be in a state of strong emotion that could either strengthen into anger or become more calm.

toil To work continuously.